MARK
TOBEY

By Colette Roberts

*Twelve Color Plates and Five
Black and White Illustrations*

Drawings by Mark Tobey

GROVE PRESS, INC. NEW YORK
EVERGREEN BOOKS, LTD. LONDON

MARK TOBEY

In Mark Tobey's symbolic abstractions painting and poetry are closely interwoven. Tobey's contribution to the expression of our time is all-important. In the adventure of today's plastic arts, doing is deeply linked to thinking and is valueless if not related to the vast experience of felt life.

For this reason and many others, Tobey's painting exists as an entity. It brings us to the essence of the art of our time, which owes its direction both to the sum of all creative thinking since 1900 and to individual visionaries who make possible for us the realization of art as exploration of the possible. Tobey is the master of what Paris refers to as the Pacific Coast School. One of the pioneers of abstract expressionism, his leap into the informal—after having fully experienced the world of forms—convinces us both of its existence and of its urgency. The 1958 Venice Biennale acknowledged with its Grand International Prize the quality of this artist, the first American painter since Whistler to win this particular international recognition there.

This absolute that painting in our time has become, this world created by man, can rightly be

7

considered an ideogram, the only universal language we have. America for a long time took its inspiration from artistic movements abroad. Since the forties, this has no longer been true. A powerful drive has propelled American painting away from former trends. The current concept of space and the influence of the Orient were instrumental in its evolution. Tobey's painting has developed in the aura of his deep sensitivity to the Oriental influence; his work is a synthesis in which East and West merge harmoniously. Deeply conscious of the importance of these two roots, Tobey has chosen to live in Seattle where he has the opportunity to experience the presence of the Orient; but his choice of the Orient is not a rejection of the Occident. According to him, until recently, America had been focusing only upon Europe, and should now recognize her geographic position and "turn her attention equally toward Asian art. All this is distinctly related to our artistic evolution."

Michel Tapié, the French art critic, in his book, *Un Art Autre* (1952), had already stated that *the importance of Tobey could never be stressed enough....For us, art movements and trends are no longer of prime interest; what matters*

*are those all too rare individuals of authentic
value. This has led us to new concepts of
power, duty, and living.*

Whereas the development of art is expressed on a
world-wide scale, America has become the cross-
road where the most profound problems, expressed
in the inevitable interaction of the Oriental and
the Occidental, confront each other. Indeed, the
quality of Tobey's work received a warm reception
from well-informed Parisian artistic circles. As
early as 1949, Jeanne Bucher had offered the artist
a one-man show. A quick examination of both
French and American avant-gardes preceding this
date will show their respective evolution and will
enable us to trace Tobey's contribution to the
world of art.

Abstraction, like cubism, was born in the early
part of the century. For many years following its
birth, painting grew in and out of geometric abstraction. In the early thirties, the international
world of abstract painting as shown at the Galerie
Pierre ranged from Mondrian to Miró, including
members of the Bauhaus, Kupka, and the American John Ferren. An analysis of the 1937-1953
period appears in *Bilan de l'Art Actuel*, published
under the direction of Robert Lebel. Indeed, as

early as 1936, "Témoignage," a group of French painters, advocated an esthetic credo in which the inside image had priority over the world of appearances. This group claimed kinship with the free teaching of Bissière and voiced their conviction through Manessier: "Nonfigurative painting gives the painter the opportunity to discover his essence and to be able to express his inner self." Ten years later Bissière defined his own position: his painting had become *"un besoin d'effusion."* Painters as varied as Wols, Fautrier, Dubuffet, Soulages, Mathieu plunged into the "informel." In Paris the general evolution of painting has prepared the terrain for a total acceptance of Tobey. Before 1949 too in America "authentic individuals" conquered large surfaces, devouring space with the appetite of a minotaur in a painterly way. "The American Abstract Artists" group, which represented a cross-section of abstract painters and sculptors, was organized in 1936. Isolated artists and others in recently formed groups were such painters as Gorky, Pollock, Rothko, Still, Gottlieb, Baziotes and, toward 1945, De Kooning, Motherwell, etc. The name "abstract expressionism" was given to this trend which was characterized by its vehement statements. A new form of surrealism was expressed by abstractions painted with a tremendous physical vitality.

Following a parallel evolution, but with a different scale, Tobey showed an *esprit de mesure*, a sense of moderation, which endeared him to those frightened by the aggressive quality of his more romantic colleagues. There is, perhaps, a new aspect of a classic humanism in Tobey which singles him out of the general current of abstract expressionism. However, a painting is not evaluated by the space it occupies on the wall, and the elastic definition of *Un Art Autre* applies to any form of truly creative plastic expression.

The history of the impressionist movement has established the areas that actually linked each member of the group to the others, as well as to artists who preceded them. In this way, nothing is closer to Tobey's work perhaps than that of another American "Nabi," Mark Rothko, also represented at the Venice Biennale in a huge retrospective exhibition. Painters of the infinitely expanded and the infinitely small meet, for they both show their awareness of man's destiny while facing the immensity of the American desert and the maze of the city jungles of mechanical and industrial superstructures. In each one can be found the humility of man whose incantation was born of solitude and is a sign of the transcendental.

What the Paris art world may have found particularly appealing in Tobey's work is the subtle quality of his color, and a synthesis where romanticism and classicism contribute to create a sense of achievement. The full implication of Tobey's work is valid not only because it is a faithful reflection of his time but also because it is an expression of his intuition of new worlds, of new perspectives. Some of his titles—*Outer Space, The Edge of August, Forms Follow Man*—illustrate his approach to a new reality.

Should one draw the conclusion that the esthetic value of the work is totally dependent upon its ideological content, or that the reading of it into the work made by the artist, and ourselves later, is all-essential? This would be too simple: a well-informed listener may have a thorough technical understanding of a musical composition without sensing its creative motivation, just as two human beings may know each other thoroughly and never be in love. The knowledge of a language will make communication possible. It may or may not be the first step toward a deep understanding. The intuitive part of understanding, like communion, will remain metaphysical and essentially subjective.

Doubtless in Tobey's work the symbolism of his canvases deals with the search for the infinite, which has a philosophical implication as well as a painterly expression. To present the man may bring us closer to the work if we limit ourselves to the climate that determines its quality. But it would be a mishandling of the problems of painting and of the painter Tobey to create specific links between the man and the work. It would be assuming that painting has no law of its own and that the magic inherent in the life of the canvas never made itself felt, whereas from the moment the contact is established between the canvas and the painter a dialogue takes place involving them much more deeply than the literarily inclined amateur can imagine. Furthermore, if this were not so, the painting would have no message and would remain surface work. To explain technically the work of a painter is to use his production and point of view to explain one's consciousness of the problems he seems to deal with and, in fact, our interpretation of these may well be correct, and correspond to those of the painter in general. But the struggle of an artist with a given canvas will always remain a mystery. A picture may be an answer, it can also be a question. In any event, each valid artist seeks an order, postulates the whole cosmos giving man a new situation in the universe, re-establishing a confidence that may give birth to hope.

But before we enter the thought of the painter, let us recall a few important dates in Mark Tobey's life.

LANDMARKS IN
MARK TOBEY'S EXPERIENCE

1890 Born December 11, in Centerville, Wisconsin.

Early years spent in Trempealeau, a small Wisconsin town on the Mississippi.

1906 Family moves to suburbs of Chicago.

1908 Forced to abandon studies after two years of high school. Takes various jobs: office boy in a steel mill, work in the clothing industry, on pulp magazines.

Draws constantly in his free time, sketching from any available model.

Attends Saturday classes at the Art Institute of Chicago for a time.

Admires such masters of the day as John Singer Sargent and Zuloaga.

As he strives for technical skill on all levels of the applied arts and illustration, the role of creative art takes on new meaning for him.

1911 Goes to New York. Divides his time between Chicago and New York.

Fashion design drawing for magazines in both cities provides material security.

1912 ⎱ Becomes dissatisfied with the stylization
1917 ⎰ of commercial designing, begins drawing from life.

Experiments with changes of the human figure in motion and at rest.

Specializes in portraiture.

1917 First exhibition at the Knoedler Gallery, New York, showing charcoal portraits of such celebrities as Mary Garden and Governor Bell.

1918 After World War I, attracted to Persian religion, Baha'i, extolling aspirations toward unification of all life, and peace. Travels to western United States.

1922 Settles in Seattle, Washington, and begins two-year teaching assignment at the Cornish School.

Makes many drawings inspired by local scenes.

Meets Chinese painter, Teng Kwei, who initiates him into the methods of Chinese calligraphy and brush stroke.

1926 Develops new outlook on esthetics. Eager for new experience, travels through Europe and Near East, settling for short time in France.

1927 Returns to Seattle, to experience mixed influences from Europe and Asia.

1930 Departs for England, as artist-in-residence at Dartington Hall School in Devonshire. Travels extensively during next seven years with England as his fixed residence.

1931 Trip to Mexico.

1934 Travels through China and Japan. Studies calligraphy in China, spending several months in Shanghai with Teng Kwei's family. In Japan stays at Zen Buddhist monastery.

1935 First one-man museum showing, Seattle Art Museum.
During latter part of European sojourn, begins new painting technique, referred to as "white writing."

1936 Broadway Norm, *tempera on cardboard*, is first important painting using this technique. Broadway, second painting in this style.

1939 Return to Seattle, where he still maintains permanent residence.

1942   Marian Willard, New York gallery owner,
       visits Seattle and takes some of his work
       back to New York.
       Metropolitan Museum of Art, New
       York, acquires Broadway, a purchase
       prize in "Artists for Victory" exhibition.

1944   First one-man gallery show, Willard Gal-
       lery, New York, qualified by Clement
       Greenberg: "...one of the few original
       contributions to ╱
       Marian Willard be╱
       York representati╱
       man shows in 1945.
       1950, 1951, 1953, 195╱
       The Museum of Moder╱
       purchases Threading Lig╱

1945   Rummage Sale awarded╱
       Pepsi-Cola competition.

1946   Included in the important "Fc╱
       Americans" exhibition at The M╱
       of Modern Art, New York, whi╱
       quires Remote Fields the followin╱

1948   Represented in the United States ╱   ╱
       of the Venice Biennale.

1950   Participates in three-man exhib╱   ╱t
       Portland Museum of Art.

18

CONSTELLATION - 7 ½ × 10 ¾'' - 1954 - Tempera - Private collection.

INTERSECTION - 9 × 12" - 1954 - Tempera.

PACIFIC CIRCLE - 44 × 34 ¾" - 1956 - Tempera
Collection Ira Haupt, New York.

MEDITATIVE SERIES No 9 - 15 ¾ × 10 ½'' - 1954 - Tempera
Collection Miss Dorothea Speyer.

Gothic *receives two prizes, for modern and representational art, at Henry Art Gallery.*

1951 *Comprehensive retrospective exhibition organized at the California Palace of the Legion of Honor, San Francisco, by Dr. Jermayne MacAgy. After circulating through western museums, show presented by Whitney Museum of American Art, New York.*
Represented in exhibition of American art, Berlin and Charlottenburg, Germany.

1952 *Work shown in "American Vanguard" exhibit prepared by Sidney Janis, at Galerie de France, Paris. (At Sidney Janis Gallery, New York, in 1951.)*

1953 *In Second International Art Exhibition, circulated through Japan and Honolulu.*

1954 *One-man show at the Otto Seligman Gallery, which becomes his exclusive representative in Seattle.*

1954 ⎫ *Travels in Europe, participating in exhibi-*
1955 ⎭ *tions in galleries in Paris (Galerie Rive Droite, Galerie Stadler), Rome (Spazio), and in museums in several countries.*

Selections from The Museum of Modern Art collection, New York, circulated through Paris, Zurich, Barcelona, The Hague, Vienna, Belgrade.

1955 *One-man show at Institute of Contemporary Arts, London.*

First one-man show in Paris at Galerie Jeanne Bucher, enthusiastically received by the international art world.

Retrospective exhibition, Art Institute of Chicago, where Window *had been awarded the M. V. Kohnstamm Prize the previous year.*

Represented in III São Paulo Bienal, American Group.

Shown in Third International Art Exhibition, Japan.

One-man gallery shows in Seattle, San Francisco, Los Angeles.

1956 *Recipient of the Fine Arts Medal, American Institute of Architects.*

Elected to membership in the National Institute of Arts and Letters.

Awarded first prize in "American Section" in first Guggenheim International Award selection.

28

Represented by "The City" theme paintings in United States section, Venice Biennale.

1957   Work shown in Third International Exhibition of Contemporary Art in India.

1958   Selection of 35 paintings at XXIX Venice Biennale awarded Grand International Prize for Painting given by the Municipality of Venice.

Sumi painting, Symbols over the West, shown in Carnegie International, Pittsburgh.

Recipient of first "Art in America" Award.

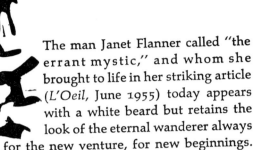

The man Janet Flanner called "the errant mystic," and whom she brought to life in her striking article (*L'Oeil,* June 1955) today appears with a white beard but retains the look of the eternal wanderer always ready for the new venture, for new beginnings. He confesses that "unless you renounce, you cannot stop, you cannot rest, you have to keep going." Let us glance at the man, witness his smiling blue eyes always close to laughter, the youthful look of one eager to know and to play. His early association with nature and open-air existence, as well as his struggles to survive poverty, gave Tobey's beginnings a shade of wisdom through the confidence they conveyed.

Every one of Tobey's biographers insists on the part played by the Orient in his creative process. Kochnitsky states in *Quadrum,* 1957...

> *everyone agrees, that...Tobey had introduced into the Occidental painting of our time the elements, the technics, and the processes of Chinese painting...pictorial discoveries...concept of a vibrating Space corresponding to the Great Void of Ch'an's neo-Buddhism...as many adaptations, essential ways of the art*

32

of painting used for almost 12 centuries by Chinese artists...

Kochnitsky adds: "...Time has come to separate Tobey's work from the literary legend that people like to wrap it in."
Indeed Tobey has experienced the thought of the Orient and has assimilated its lessons, but his art is never derivative, never a copy of Oriental models. It is an absorption and an identification with the Orient on the level of poetry. It somewhat brings to mind the story of the poet Léon-Paul Fargue who mentioned a Monsieur Hubert de l'Institut, a bum who gloried in sleeping under the Pont des Arts and who adopted this title which he felt his privilege—and his superiority over his colleagues—bestowed upon him by the neighboring Institute. Why the comparison? Tobey and Hubert share a common trait: they are poets and make what they respect their own.
A powerful force drives Tobey toward what he feels might be a source of truth. This truth can be apparent on various levels.
On the humanitarian and humanistic level the Baha'i faith and its quest for unity seem to have brought this harmony-loving artist the "clue to an ethic of our time." Summarized in the text-

book of Baha'i principles, the teaching, first, of Bab, and then of Bahá'u'lláh was initiated in Persia in mid-19th century. It recommends the unification of all religions, however diverse, the reconciliation of religion and science stemming from the same root, a search for truth. Tobey sums it up for us: "the Baha'i or world order of Bahá'u'lláh is a universal concept of a new world." The dynamics of this new vision once realized— which naturally took several years—brought forth such paintings as *World Egg*, *Threading Light*, *Arena of Civilization*, and others, "all symbolic signs of a new spirit of unity." As concerns Zen Buddhism, imported from China by the meditative Zen sect in the 12th century "deeply modified Japanese thinking." Tobey has an intuitive Zen sense of existence that harmonizes with his Quaker heritage. He refers us to Watt's book, *The Way of Zen*, but does not wish to comment on Zen. That Tobey's work, essentially reflexive, has found in and through the Orient a means of expressing the inexpressible—has found a language —is a certitude.

His dedication to the eternal does not do away with the particular. The city and its neon signs are among many experiences whose immediacy he perceives with a sensitive Occidental approach, almost prescient. What characterizes best this wanderer is the great ease with which he adjusts to surroundings and people without ever losing that which is Tobey. He enjoys conversations and, in general, communication.

During our many meetings, whether in Paris or New York, alone or with others, Soulages, for example, we noticed his solid adherence to that which is closely or remotely linked to his convictions. He appears to be sure of himself, sure of his universe, complaining of endless small troubles without really being affected by them. Meanwhile he is ready to capture the worthwhile, the amusing. Seated at a Paris café terrace, Wéber's especially, he looks at the crowd walking leisurely and at the trees, which play such an important part in the planning of the city. Strolling along, he admires the vestiges of the past that punctuate Paris and enchant his wanderings. "They know how to live," he remarks. This sympathy which makes him feel as one with his ambiance is an essential part of his luggage as a traveler.

In New York, where success hits him first as a pleasant surprise, and then appears to him as a dangerous trap, he enjoys walking miles, stimulated by the human anthill, noticing with nostalgia on the way the disappearance of familiar places. For much is torn down in New York. Tobey fears the lack of the past, not because he has more use for it than for the present, but because the taken-for-granted makes it possible to rest a while. The taken-for-granted of a place is like a harbor a man needs to establish his own scale of values, to dream, and to regain his consciousness of the ego without being continually caught by the newness of the outside world. This arrest makes it possible to keep track of landmarks that retrace the succession of selves linked with the memory of the object. "There can be no consciousness of the present," says Tobey, "if one destroys the past." Because his thinking is essentially based on the principle of evolution there is a refusal of revolution, of a break in the flow of images, a refusal of the type of disintegration which is destruction instead of absorption of the old by the new through an additive process. But the dynamism of the new seduces him nevertheless. The very concept of the City "one-world" intrigues him. No one better than he was able to re-create the modern city with its large surfaces of glass where daylight hits and splashes in what may seem, according to seasons, ice or fire. Yes, he is moved by this bubbling world, where men struggle or float like amoebae in a drop of water. Reflections of night, too, fascinate him. Luminous streams dig through the sky and the ground, the neon sign imprints its wavy seal through dark and shadows as a symbol of man's triumph over night. It is fitting that Tobey's concern for life should be stirred by urbane agglomerations where destinies are made or unmade, where lives grow parallel, lives started elsewhere, lives speaking every language, lives heavy with all atavisms. This rhythm of New York City—Tobey knows how to make us aware of it, through his nervous and quick brush stroke, which never describes but which creates an awareness through the quality of the calligraphy. Vibration, pulsation of life, affirmations of gesture as well as painterly thinking, quest for unity, for domination through inner discipline, for the reflection of a motion-mad world, explosive and dangerous, reflection in which the artist has introduced order—such is the work of Tobey for us. His retrospective exhibition at the Venice Biennale by invitation in 1958 met with an enthusiastic press. Françoise Choay, who had already spoken of the new perspective opened by Tobey's work

when he had his one-man show in Paris (Jeanne
Bucher, 1955) wrote (*L'Oeil*, September 1955)
that his

> *careful signs are never arbitrary, nor can they*
> *be linked to any stereotype...through their*
> *existence, categories of reflections suddenly*
> *become attuned to the order of the world.*

Enthusiastic, too, Alain Jouffroy (*Arts*, June 18,
1958) described this acuteness of vision which
situates Tobey at the very edge of perfection and
marveled at the

> *freedom with which he uses his means...the*
> *continual oscillation between the cosmic and*
> *the intellectual, between external and inner*
> *life, between the infinitely great and the in-*
> *finitely small.*

Visiting him in his spacious apartment in an old
patrician mansion, one is struck by the barren
look of this New York camping arrangement. Indeed, Tobey camps here, as he resides in Seattle.
The three large rooms of this apartment seem
even larger than they are, as Tobey has chosen to
line up the furniture against the walls. Somewhat
like an ambulatory, the void invites to meditation

YELLOW HARVEST - 36 × 42'' - 1958 - Willard Gallery Collection.

TATTOOD - 6 ½ × 10'' - 1958 - Collection of the artist.

and certainly forms an accompaniment for Tobey's walk to and fro.

Does Tobey subscribe to Tapié's reference to the words of Saint John of the Cross: "to go where you know not, go by a way you know not"? Tobey: "I have to walk when I think."

Without subsconscious faith, St. John of the Cross would not have started the journey. His quest leads him toward where he knows not by a way he knows not. It does not necessarily follow that the quest is, or is not, fulfilled— the quest being an inner condition related to subconscious faith. What matters most is keeping the eyes open for experience in new directions. Perhaps the Orient is inclusive of what we term the accidental. The accidental can lead one back toward the conscious again if accepted and used; it can lead to art.

Stressing this experience on all levels, Tobey continues:

The old Chinese used to say, "It is better to feel a painting than to look at it." So much today is only to look at. It is one thing to paint a picture and another to experience it, and in attempting to find on what level one accepts

this experience, one discovers what one sees
and on what level the discovery takes place.
Christopher Columbus left in search of one
world and discovered another.

When Tobey looks at a cup, he is not interested
by the reference to the object, but by the experience of that object. He passes by the concept of
the cup *per se* to reach its inner surface and the
space it engulfs. Running his finger around the
inner circumference and the space it engulfs, he
describes this area. Through intuition, and intuition only, this new aspect of the real can be conquered, the taken-for-granted which used to be
the inner and unknown world has now become
all-important, whereas the identity, the shell of
the object is now taken for granted.
That a work of art should be an apprehension of
the universe, that a qualitative element, by definition metaphysical, magical too, should intervene
so that the message reaches us, is of course true
whenever the actuality of a work is felt. In her
thoughtful book on 12th-century Taoist painting,
Nicole Vandier-Nicolas stresses this quality, and
we welcome her citation of Souriau:

Art is an instaurative activity...the sum of

*steps oriented and motivated which aim to
lead a being from nothingness or from an
initial chaos to complete existence, singular
and concrete, expressing itself in indubitable
presence.*

"Instauration" for Tobey starts with his consciousness of an infinite world, the Zen Buddhist
attitude which conditions an essentially natural
behavior, and a refusal to give to the universe
visual boundaries other than those dictated by an
intuition of quality. Tobey refuses to give in to
the quantitative. As for the academism born of
the new concept of space, Tobey insists that

*the cult of space can become as dull as that of
the object. The dimension that counts for the
creative person is the space he creates within
himself. This inner space is closer to the infinite than the other, and it is the privilege of
a balanced mind—and the search for an equilibrium is essential—to be as aware of inner
space as he is of outer space. If he ventures in
one, and neglects the other, man falls off his
horse and the equilibrium is broken.*

In other words, the individual would then cease
to look into the questions which make of his act

an art, a creation. *Presence* is not only determined by the answer but is also expressed by the quality of the *question.*

The questions the painter asks himself doubtless vary, and not all can be either answered or foreseen. What seems fairly apparent with Tobey is a combination of a time-space-light element somewhat reminiscent of what happens when, looking at the sky, you are both conscious of the sun hiding behind the moving cloud, and of areas of light and shadow. One is conscious too that this is not permanent: in time the cloud will move away into space. Technically, although the painter wishes to go forward, he does it without rejecting all of a plastic past—if only to retain the essence of visual experience: what is left when one has forgotten most things.

Asked about his teaching, Tobey expressed his feeling that

> *the simplest form of teaching is to start a person on the plane of his imagination. This discloses his powers—or lack of powers—of observation. His consciousness or lack stimulates his observation, which in turn stimulates his retentive memory, and unites with imagination in the next attempt. This approach to*

44

teaching would appear very slow but it is a much truer path than the recipe methods taught by lazy teachers.

To enable the pupil to find his way through new visual experiences, investigation of the past (the past that is relevant to our time) will prove an essential addenda. Study of Giotto, Rembrandt, El Greco, Cézanne, the early Braque, the Picasso of analytic cubism—as many sources of information that can be carefully deciphered by the art student to his greatest profit. This is all linked to development of observation leading to the act of painting. For Tobey, teaching was not just a job —it was, and still is for him, an "act of energy" to the same extent as painting is. It offered—for he teaches little now—the possibility of communicating, of sharing his discoveries of the moment with the same fascination a boy has when he empties his pockets at night, full of the unpredictable treasures collected during the adventure of the day. Teaching is communion. Tobey has no faith in "recipes," and aims at helping the student find his own self, his own direction. This reminds one of Bissière's teaching (also in the thirties), whose conclusion was, "When all is said, I can do nothing for you, for only the heart is all-important." This quality of dedication in all Tobey's endeavors is also stressed by Michel Seuphor in his description of Tobey's art (*Dictionnaire de l'Art Abstrait*, 1958):

Nostalgia of delicate scents, of interiority. The inner reserve of Klee or Tobey reaches more deeply into us than that of other artists because true eloquence is in the heart, and the heart is a seed that matures slowly.

The evolution of Tobey's work, although marked by definite key exhibitions, does not follow any systematic development. His themes are worked in different ways at different times and are interwoven like those of a symphony.

The first one-man show at the Willard Gallery in New York in 1944 featured a variety of works such as *E Pluribus Unum*, where the human figure was still a prevailing element, even when his "White Writing" was incorporated in these *Figures Caught in Light*. His *Two Men* (1941), in the Portland Museum, are portrait-like images of fishermen caught in subtle moonbeams. Now in the Seattle Museum, *Forms Follow Man* (1942) uses a single uninterrupted line molding bodies with a Boccioni-like staccato and pushing them away as swirling wind would dead leaves. Epoch-making too was his 1945 "War, City, Indian, Religious" exhibition at the Willard Gallery, for which the late Lyonel Feininger wrote in his preface to the catalogue:

> *Like poetry and music, his pictures have the time element; they unfold their contents gradually. With an active imagination they*

have to be approached, read, and their sym-
bols interpreted. They reveal their tenor if one
listens with the inner ear...

This show, like a vast orchestration, featured man and his credos analyzed on various levels leading toward unity. Typical of this period, *Drums, Indians and the Word of God* (1944, 48 x 33", tempera) presents a Lilliputian man surrounded by gigantic images: man seen as a prey to his symbols. Another landmark of the painter's evolution, *Arena of Civilization* (1947), is a Baha'i painting. The 1949 theme dealt with man and his patterns of culture in a wide range of symbolic subject matter. It included too his *City Paintings*. Typical of this was his *Awakening Night*. Describing the 1949 presentation, the American critic Henry McBride wrote: "Abstract variations on minuscule symbols repeated over and over with a Bach-like building-up into a massive composition that in turn yields endless matter for brooding contemplation." This description suits equally well the *Meditative Series* exhibition of 1954. Two examples of this particularly subtle development can be seen here. The recent sumi exhibition "Space Rituals" (1957) showed a new departure—described later—with a new medium,

48

an escapade into the unknown, one of those voyages Tobey never fears.

The main contribution of Tobey to his time is his ceaseless attempt—and his success—to harmonize two seemingly contradictory worlds: the Orient ruled by intuition, and the Occident ruled by an empirical description of nature. In his pictures, the quiet range of his palette takes him through all the stages of lyrical abstraction, using the scale of Lilliput rather than that of Gulliver. His Sumi paintings, inkwashes in black and white, and his last mural, are exceptions to his usual scale.

Here the rhythm of his black sumi ink stroke takes new directions and new dimensions and is more obviously related to the Chinese and particularly Japanese tradition. The lashing of the stroke, the splashing of the ink, are nevertheless as controlled here as in the minute temperas, and the pendulum-like motion goes from the relative to the absolute, always finding an equilibrium between the descriptive and the intuitive. Sometimes the human face emerges from the dark inking, for Tobey never completely forsakes the human form, as if man's symbol was a reassuring element, an oasis of rest in this quest for the unknown.

The whole Sumi series is referred to as *Space Rituals,* and should not be interpreted as the cult of space but as a rapport in which space and rite combine in a mystical act. Possibly his *Symbols over the West,* a center piece in his 1957 show at the Willard Gallery and shown at the Pittsburgh Carnegie International, 1958, can be considered the most expressive plastic embodiment of this thinking. These smoke-like symbols read like totemic images reaching toward the sky, while back of them a subtle and quietly radiant light suggests unlimited space. One feels through the whole composition a deep concern for the transcendental. Other Sumi inkwashes are landscape studies (light caught between heavy foliage, suggestions of clearings, etc.) all handled in the Eastern fashion. This gesture is linked to the impression received from the outside world. The Sumi series does not characterize the whole of Tobey's work, but is a valuable addendum. These inkwashes are bold acts as compared to the careful illumination and technique of his reflective temperas.

One hesitates to use the word "illumination," since this applies to a decorative and an illustrative process, totally foreign to Tobey's interest.

Nevertheless, his minutely calculated brush stroke and the ideas embodied in the doing relate somewhat to, we might say, illumination of a text simultaneously dreamed, written, and painted by the artist. These illuminations are part of what could be referred to as Tobey's traveling notebook. Never shown to the public, these small temperas (they do not exceed twelve inches in length) are semi-abstractions—almost totally non-objective—but are referred to by the painter as the impressions of Paris Sketches. One is surprised to hear names of well-known places, for they correspond to *elsewhere*. These minute Tobeys are like so many flying carpets which take us into a world Tobey conquered before he could take us along on his venture into an intuitive *real*. But Tobey has shown recently that whatever the scale, the image is his. Finishing a mural for February, 1959, he chose to leave his usual microcosm for large symbols of flat color. White, dark blue, brown, on a gray background, his forms emerge like collages, creating their own space, and suggesting somewhat a pendulum-like oscillation, a sense of the relative that is quite his own, which here owes nothing to the painter's usual brush stroke.

The truth which he reaches at different times and on different levels can be felt, and Tobey does wish to communicate. Aggression with its negative aspect never seems to interest him. To assert today's findings he does not have to negate yesterday's affirmations. He accepts every aspect of experience as a means. In her preface to the Whitney Museum retrospective exhibition in 1951, Dr. Jermayne MacAgy referred to criticisms of Tobey for experimenting too much. She cites his answer: "...I thrust forward into space as science and the rest do." There is never a refusal in Tobey's work, but a succession of acceptances in harmony with every stage of his evolution. He is deeply penetrated by the requirements of life and the creative process, and the esthetics he rejects stop existing from the very minute he has exhausted their potential. He does not need to run yesterday down. For that reason, too, rivalry does not concern him. His art is peacefully, serenely, "*autre*," different. When André Masson, in his article, "Painting of the Essential," in *Quadrum*, 1956, analyzed the art of the Orient, he stressed that

the essential for the Zen painter is in no way similar to what the Occidental painter means by this terminology. For the Chinese, or his

Japanese colleague, this means a manner of
being in the deepest sense and not, as for us,
a manner of doing. For them it means fusion
in the life of the cosmos, and for us a way of
summing up.

Tobey is a mixture of both. He owes to his Occidental background the summing-up quality of his painting, but he backs it with a partial conformity to the Oriental way of life. His summing up takes place in the "insituable," leaving an open door to all the elsewheres. No doubt Tobey could have used Klee's words (Brion, *L'Art Abstrait*): "I dream...of a work...which would embrace all the fields of the elements, of the object, of the meaningful, and of style." Klee yesterday, Tobey today, are creators of worlds.

Above all, Tobey's art is to the field of representation what a word is to the field of language. Engaged in the adventure of the "informel," his work in general frees us from the world of appearances without falling into the excesses of lyricism which hamper communication. Tobey's lyrical abstractions wish to become present, are present. And it is this *presence* which has for us become synonymous with beauty since, as Malraux wrote perceptively, presence includes beauty without defining it. Tobey knows how to communicate his presence because he wishes and knows how to attach us to his search for the *real*. At this point, one will never stress too much how far remote this real is from commonplace reality. Nor can one stress too much to what extent painting and poetry in combination can create an awareness of the real on every level.

Georges Mathieu analyzed in his *New Reincarnation of Signs* the various stages of art history, in search first of the ideal, then evolving from the ideal to the real, "from the real to the abstract, and from the abstract to the possible." It is obvious that we now enter the area of the possible. At this very point, Mathieu concludes that "after Wols and Tobey, all signs have to be re-created." We may see there that lyrical abstraction is a way of being and not a stylized approach to life, as new breeds of academism might suggest. This homage to Tobey shows the place the young avant-garde give him as they recognize in him both a contemporary and an elder.

Similarly, statements by fellow American artists stress, as did Feininger (preface to the catalogue of the exhibition at the Willard Gallery), that

Mark Tobey's pictures are not optical in the

END OF SUMMER. 1956. Tempera. 24 x 36".
Collection Galerie Beyeler, Basel

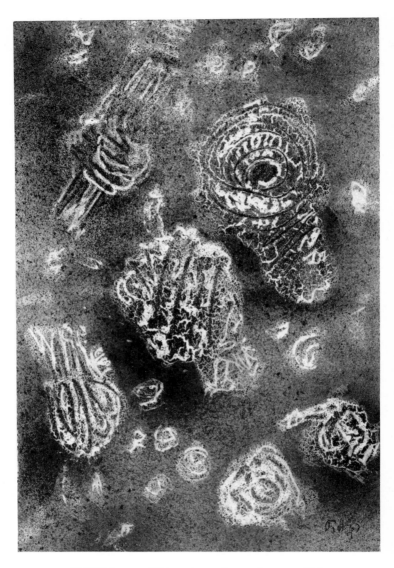

FOSSILS. 1957. Watercolor and gouache. 11 x 7¹/₂".
Collection Galerie Beyeler, Basel

THUNDERING PLAINS. 1957. Sumi ink. $23\frac{1}{2}$ x 34".
Collection Galerie Beyeler, Basel

traditional sense of painting....A painter who
for the tales he has to tell in his pictures has
created a new convention of his own; one not
yet included in the history of painting...

Indeed, the world of Tobey's beginnings was different from today's world. Nothing was set before Tobey in his youth to direct him. He had to
feel his way toward what lived and was felt within
him. Indeed what gives life to a work of art has
this in common with the embryo: it is the complete embodiment of a new life—genes and cells
may be related to the parent cells and genes; iden-
tically the new art may embody the technique of
previous art, but both can exist only if they have
a life of their own.

At a time when the masses are increasingly pre-
occupied by material achievements and the world
of appearances can be recorded by the visual arts
born from science, we have freed ourselves from
the notion that the function of plastic arts is to be
representational. It is therefore natural that artists, as prophets, delve into the unknown in their
search for truth and essence. Painting has taken
the form of visual poetry and has suddenly become *incantation*. The painter invites us to his
world and, as is true of all arts, this world grows

into an image that encompasses more than the artist's dreams; it reflects the quality of his self. Now it is the artist as a whole whom we accept or reject.

The art of Tobey vibrates, pulsates, lives.

ERRATUM

The caption for AWAKENING NIGHT
appears incorrectly under the left side of
the painting.
